DAYS OF DARK AND LIGHT

Days of Dark and Light

RECENT POEMS

David Thompson

THE HOBNOB PRESS
2021

First published in the United Kingdom in 2021 by

The Hobnob Press,
8 Lock Warehouse, Severn Road, Gloucester GL1 2GA
www.hobnobpress.co.uk

© David H. Thompson text and images, 2021

The Author hereby asserts his moral rights to be identified as the Author of the Work.

All rights reserved. No part of this publication may be reproduced, stored in a retrieval system, or transmitted in any form or by any means, electronic, mechanical, photocopying, recording or otherwise, without the prior permission of the publisher and copyright holder.

British Library Cataloguing in Publication Data
A catalogue record for this book is available from the British Library

ISBN 978-1-914407-16-1

Typeset in Adobe Garamond Pro 12/14 pt.
Typesetting and origination by John Chandler

For Daniel, Charis and Matthew

> How clear, how lovely bright,
> How beautiful to sight
>   Those beams of morning play;
> How heaven laughs out with glee
> Where, like a bird set free,
> Up from the eastern sky
>   Soars the delightful day.
>
>   A. E. Housman, *More Poems*

Acknowledgements

Several of these poems have appeared in the social media pages of Words at the Black Swan and Frome Poetry Café. Others were entered for the weekly writing challenges of the King Lear Arts Club, and were subsequently printed in the Club's email newsletter.

I'm particularly grateful to two writers who have given generous encouragement. In our regular poetry conversations, Claire Crowther has taught me much of what I've learnt over the past year and a half and offered a multitude of perceptive comments from her rich knowledge and experience as a working poet. And since the first Words at the Black Swan workshop I attended in Frome in January 2020, Crysse Morrison has been a constant inspiration, not least because of her familiarity with the classics of English poetry. Her guidance and advice have been crucial. Lastly, John Chandler of Hobnob Press has been exemplary in steering me through the various stages of publication.

Foreword

During the period from early 2020 to mid-2021, when the Covid-19 pandemic dominated much of daily life, many elements of experience were limited by an array of restrictions. Without travel, or the opportunity for everyday encounters, imagination and memory became even more important. In my case, a return to writing, and particularly to poetry, was a means of escaping or transcending the collapse of normal life. At the same time, I wanted to explore a variety of poetic forms, some of them unfamiliar, that were stimulating to attempt and seemed to match latent images and feelings. The poems that follow are the result.

Contents

I THE VIEW FROM THE GARDEN — 11

In Praise of Bees	13
Sun-Kissed Blackbird	14
Ink Black, Pale Blue	15
The Last Full Moon	17
Four Skies of Winter	18
Wilding Your Garden	19
Sparrows	20
Orchard	22
Skylines	23
The Colours of My Heart's Garden	24

II IN NATURE — 25

Autumn Painting	27
Woodland, October	28
To The Spirit of Spring on May Day	29
Four Haiku	30
What am I?	31
Butterflies Are Magic	32
A Gorgeous Butterfly	33

III IN OTHER LANDS — 35

Charcoal at the Pointe du Milier	37
Mary, by the Estuary	38
Lament	39
Supper with the Special Who	40

IV WORDS AND THE ARTS   41

Responding to 'Chaos'   43
'Fifty Bees' at the Black Swan   44
Black Swan Arts Young Open 2020   46
Embrace   47
Car Boot at Standerwick   48
Poets: A Random Pantheon   49
Every Inch A King   50
Trompe-l'oeil at Chatsworth   51
Luncheon of the Boating Party   52
Requiem: The Arts Endure   53

V JEOPARDY   55

No Child is a Lighthouse   57
We Three Camels   58
How We're Feeling on the Ark   59
Counting the Days   60
The Elections: Can Jon Win?   62

VI THE HARD YEARS   65

Self-isolation   67
Getting Ready for Zoom   68
Ten Haiku: A Sequence for the Times   69
Where Sound Should Live   71
Now   72
Let's All Grab a Jab   73
Ordinary Things To Do Again   74

I
THE VIEW FROM THE GARDEN

In Praise of Bees

Villanelle

From flower to seedhead, fertile fruiting trees;
as spring and summer follow winter's cold,
my garden cannot thrive without the bees.

I dig and plant and prune and tease
out the weeds that hurry to enfold;
from flower to seedhead, fertile fruiting trees.

Seedlings green the soil, take their new-found ease,
reaching skyward, timid first then bold;
my garden may not thrive without the bees.

The stems extend, the buds burst into leaves;
as rain drops stipple, sepalled blooms unfold;
from flower to seedhead, fertile fruiting trees.

Coaxed by the warmth and summoned by the breeze,
the blossoms sunbathe, brushed by powdered gold;
my garden does not thrive without the bees.

I sniff the nectar, feel the fragrance seize
the hunters' senses, sweet hunger take hold.
From flower to seedhead, fertile fruiting trees;
my garden could not thrive without the bees.

Sun-Kissed Blackbird

A ghazal for lockdown

Sun-kissed blackbird, plant your feet in lockdown
on the song tree, incomplete in lockdown –

the prunus, once a cloud of pink each spring,
preferred to die than repeat in lockdown.

I need your evening melody to drown
the sullen percussive beat in lockdown.

Your voice pulses as the lyrics ripple,
their patterned notes of love sweet in lockdown.

Your bill gleams gold as the sky opens
to the sun; hidden beauties meet in lockdown.

Like polished coal your sable feathers shine;
help me breathe, my heart replete in lockdown.

Ink Black, Pale Blue

The ink spill smudging
the eastern sky slips
its black horizon,
clears to shoaled pale blue:
a time for rainbows.

Flat westward, half-sunk,
the sun cuts willow,
paints silver birches,
flares red ripe apples,
gilds the tall roses.

I click my tongue
to call companions
and toss scraps sky-high
to fan as they fall
into low-mown grass.

One, then the other,
my two crows glide down.
They sense a presence,
pause on a dead branch,
drop light to the lawn.

Alert they peck, strut,
necks tensile, wings poised,
while from the dark reeds
the shape-shifting cat
slinks belly-stalking.

The crows feign languor,
push away skyward,
scorning a creature
that kills, not for need –
for the hell of it.

The Last Full Moon

This was no night to slip unseen into the New Year:
the full moon's searchlight split the dark,
shadows black-edged as gravestones,
ice blades welded on grass stems,
frost aglint on the railings' angles.

So we flew up into the blazing night, struck
a tangent to the vast moon's rainbow ring,
strolled brazenly across the sky,
skin to skin through the stage-lit gateway,
counting the stars as we passed beyond.

Next morning, next year, the balcony frosted white,
the sun broke the horizon over Cley Hill.
Hot light hit the windows to scour our night-numb eyes
and skimmed the levelled world
to finger unlit paintings on the farthest wall.

Four Skies of Winter

Late January. Sun hits the fruit trees.
Apple points split and bare their velvet lips;
tight pears and plums sleep latent in the freeze,
shy cherries clench the secrets of their tips.

Then comes the rain. Sparse flowers sprig the shrubs.
Viburnum drips in winter white, pink-dipped,
camellias flaunt in crimson from their tubs,
wet hazels dangle catkins, twigs green-tipped.

A final blaze as light makes way for dark.
The North beds down, its shift as backdrop done;
the South's a storm-edged ridge of blacks and greys;
to Eastward, double rainbows trace their arc;
to West, the stagy splash of diving sun –
the closing day's four weathers and four skies.

Wilding Your Garden

Look round and see which native trees might grow,
what flowers and shrubs would thrive by right;
what blooms could lure loud insects in the sun,
what scents for moths to track by night.

Think too of wilding lawn and unloved ground
with floral mixes, herbs and weeds.
Imagine meadow, pollen-rich for bees,
that draws birds in to raid the seeds.

Create a pond, place reeds for dragonflies,
aquatic plants for newts and frogs.
Let squirrels climb up high to tease the crows,
leave gaps to squeeze through for hedgehogs.

Make walls for lizards, havens for slow-worms,
hedges for nesting birds and mice.
Protect the ivy where it flowers and fruits –
safe refuge, wildlife paradise.

Sparrows

We built twin raised beds two yards apart, sharp frames
of oak-slab railway sleepers, some fresh-cut,
some warped, fungoid and fissured, exact angles
so hard you'd expect an Escher illusion.

>You sat winter through,
>you greeted the spring;
>out of the hedge
>into the world.

The first bed tangles herbs in lush disorder –
mint and lovage, tarragon, thyme, marjoram,
chives and sorrel. Roots battle under the soil
while green shoots above tempt kitchen fingers.

>You don't sing tunes
>we can whistle,
>just the racket
>of spadger chirp.

The second bed's bare, dry, forked and composted,
waiting for water and the promise of seeds;
a powdery playground, a stranded hull
crewed by shy night cats and bold daytime birds.

Wired to party, set
on bustle and fun,
you mine the dust bath,
dishevelled, grubby,
promiscuous,
concupiscent,
tossing, tumbling,
catch as catch can.

Time's up, sparrows, no more spugsy stuff.
Nip back to cover, make way for robins,
cuter, queuing in the brambly viburnum,
dusty worms already dangling in their eyes.

Orchard

Each year the ring of trees progresses,
swallowing strips of lawn, breaking taboos.
It's an amicable rainbow; I don't feel cornered
on the terrace. They're edging space:
soon they'll spill from the stalls and become
actors, owning the stage.
For now they're my watchful choir,
waiting for the upbeat.

Serbian quinces join the English apples,
plums and pears, debating damsons',
gages' and cherries' place in the arc.
New varieties, embedded, staked, composted,
grow diverse, resilient, resistant:
they're shaping a tribe, more than the sum.

The mesh of roots beneath the ground
negotiates, builds an alliance,
commits to being an orchard, together
planning buds, flowers and fruit.

Such pacts make failed Eden jealous:
gales thrash the blossom,
harsh rains pelt the unformed fruit;
but the young shoots endure.

Skylines

The birches pause their bowing
to west or east; the sky's lustre
hints the sun's changing to rain
as late clouds muster.

Aligned along the terrace,
the coloured spikes of dusk-scented roses;
before the pond, flared with yellow flag,
tall grass interposes.

Crows perch on the skyline
of the weeping willow's apse,
drop down to probe
the day's strewn scraps.

Along the hedge top, silhouetted pigeons
pick their way, homing to improbably
slung nests. Blackbirds, distrusting the quiet,
settle warily.

A fly dots the foam line
of an evening mug of beer,
greedy to claim its share
of the sweet malt lure.

The Colours of My Heart's Garden

The descending syllables of a nonet

Red admirals and ripe strawberries,
Orange-tips on pink lady-smock,
Yellow sunburst of brimstones,
Green hairstreaks, gold gages,
Blue tits, damselflies,
Indigo plums,
Violets:
Rainbow –
You.

II
IN NATURE

Autumn Painting

When you sent the painting
I didn't expect you'd touch me,
didn't expect
this lost body to respond.

Was it the forest, you beside me,
and your voice's autumn colour?
These are the golden trees
that map the labyrinth.

Woodland, October

Ruled in shaded verticals,
beech trunks, bark squirrel-skid smooth,
prop the still-green forest cap.

Rhododendrons pattern the fog,
ferns feather in tight bouquets,
fungi exhale their ripe musk.

Deer slots carve the matted crust
spacing bracken umbrellas
where unnamed insects bustle.

Plumbline perfect, the columns
project all motion skywards,
timber outshining built stone.

To The Spirit of Spring on May Day

In homage to William Wordsworth

This is your peerless day, beloved Spring,
when warming sun gilds Flora's wakening.
Snowdrops and daffodils have danced and gone,
blackthorn's dazzling banks of white are done,
and pioneer April turns to bluebell May
as pear and apple join the cherries' play.
Orange-tips roam in search of lady-smock
and saxifrage starts buds upon the rock.
Sweet rain swells brooks cascading down the dales
where plunging otters sport with grey wagtails.
The tiny wren, mighty in melody,
outdoes the songthrush in its rhapsody;
willow catkins scatter their hasty dust
and hazels nurture cob-nuts as they must.
Craggy rowans unfurl their tight-bunched fists
of blossom; their feathered foliage resists
the hillside breezes parting earth and sky,
while oaks' green castles vaunt their majesty.
In every creature, every flaunting flower,
now Nature celebrates the fecund hour.

Four Haiku

Moorland stream

By the stepping stones
smoke curls from soft-blown embers;
tickled trout for tea.

Llandudno story

Goats from the Great Orme
leave their crags for empty streets:
tasty front gardens.

On Collard Hill

Underground, Large Blues
chew ant grubs, emerge to seek
tight buds of wild thyme.

For the pollinators

Ribbons of flowers,
nectar-rich, rim the cornfields.
Bees buzz, birds' wings flash.

What am I?

A riddle in kennings

Scale-winged soarer
Sun adorer
Zigzag flighter
Soft alighter

Hedgerow rider
Woodland glider
Meadow surfer
Sheep-grazed turfer

Blossom searcher
Petal percher
Pollen nuzzler
Nectar guzzler

Butterflies Are Magic

Acrostic

Beyond the wild garden there's a kingdom
Under sunlit spring skies, where fantasy
Takes to golden wings as Brimstones sweep past,
Tortoiseshells trip on Peacocks' ecstasy.

Emerging Orange-tips, Whites, Speckled Woods,
Red Admirals strut in festive panoply;
Fritillaries trapeze through shaded glades,
Lone Hairstreaks sky-dance in the canopy.

In time for summer flings, Painted Ladies
Enchant majestic Purple Emperors;
Swallowtails break out from their fenland haunts
And Commas swoop to do their nettle tours.

Roving Ringlets, Heaths, Walls and Meadow Browns
Ease from stem to stem and bloom to bloom;
Migrating Clouded Yellows nectar here,
And Skippers bask and joust and dart and zoom.

Glinting Coppers, heavens of Azure Blue:
Imagine this Pearl-Bordered paradise –
Could dreams be lovelier than butterflies?

A Gorgeous Butterfly

A fatras, reformed

If there's one thing that makes my day,
it's seeing a gorgeous butterfly.
If there's one thing that makes my day,
it's catching colours with each ray
and watching sunshine paint the sky:
Adonis blues skimming the hay
while skippers lightly land to lay;
painted ladies, nectaring by,
red admirals, no scale awry,
marbled whites in two-tone array,
each peacock's wing a halcyon eye.
If there's one thing drives cares away,
it's seeing a gorgeous butterfly.

III
IN OTHER LANDS

Charcoal at the Pointe du Milier

The Pointe du Milier is on the coastal path west of the fishing port of Douarnenez (Finistère)

I'll start at the Moulin de Kériolet, climb down
past the leat and water wheel to the lower chamber,
skirt the carved mass of the millstones,
smell the goodness of the fresh-ground meal,
register the congruence of flour and bags.

Then I'll take the track to the lighthouse cottage,
cutting corners from the cliff edge, down by
animal trails mapping the maze of the thorn scrub
to the salt scent of sea and rocks and sand,
and up again to the path along the middle contour.

It's late spring, so the sun's setting north of west.
There's a turfy seat, as if made for painters;
I'll enthrone, charcoal and pad in hand,
finger and thumb soon smudgy as I
work wood grit into slabs of light and shade.

Sketched out and content, black dust spray-fixed,
I'll slide the slope back to the path,
soak in the sun-rimmed silhouette of backlit
fishing boats homing east to port,
then follow west the gold seam to the horizon.

Mary, by the Estuary

In memory of Mary Hurley

Mary,
by the estuary, this image:
you were above, profiled on the dyke;
Bella – racy lurcher manacled to your wrist –
leapt to chase an egret.
Wham! Thistledown, you angel-dived,
pancaked unhurt on the polder below.

Mary,
I never give bookmarks away,
but painted one for you: a blue boat,
hauled up on the shingle, crewed
by dogs and cats – the animals you loved;
then green clenched pines; a grey wall;
the piscatory workday sea.

Mary,
you walked with me barefoot
to the shallows of the Baie d'Audierne.
We cast your sister's ashes in the wind,
washed and swallowed by small waves.
Bella watched our wet eyes
and nuzzled your hand.

Lament

I used to make poems, write dramas and stories;
I used to make films, read plays, take to the stage;
I used to make gardens, walk mountains and valleys;
I used to make plans, meet the future head on.

I used to make journeys, speak tongues and meet strangers;
I used to make music, play flutes and sing songs;
I used to make pots, paint flowers and forests;
I used to make life work, but now you are gone.

Supper with the Special Who

Remember reading poetry by the Seine?
Steak frites for supper, strawberries and cream,
already crammed with Rimbaud and Verlaine;
a shared umbrella, dashing home to dream?
And Venice, walking till we could no more –
canals and paintings, nooks where churches hid;
a break for soft-cooked *sarde in saor,*
spaghetti laced with midnight black of squid.
To Wien for *Apfelstrudel,* coffee, cakes;
then taste *souvlaki* by the Parthenon;
frittura, sun and wine on Piedmont lakes.
But what meant most was not the food that shone:
it's where and when we ate, the special who
we ate with, and for me that's always you.

IV
WORDS AND THE ARTS

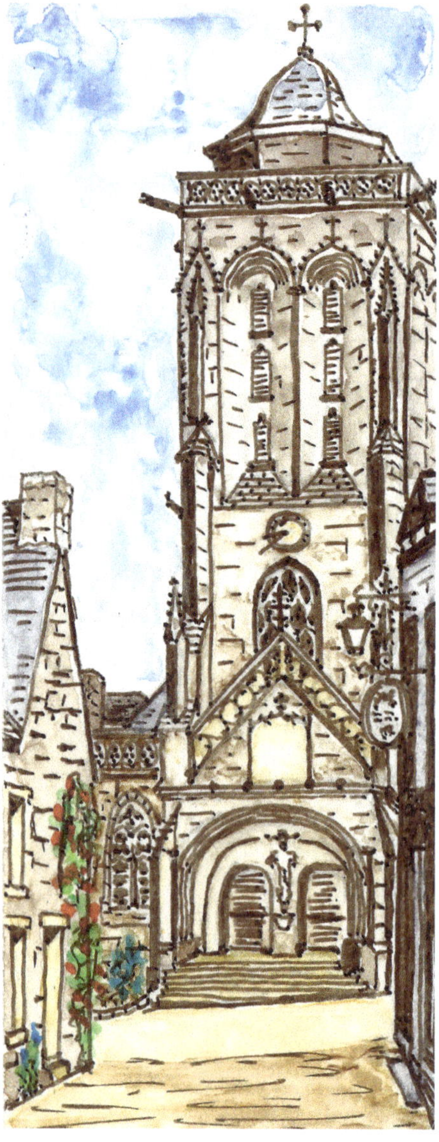

Responding to 'Chaos'

Barry Cooper's January 2020 exhibition of paintings with Eugène Ysaÿe's music at the Black Swan, Frome

'Chaos is never far from the surface'

Volcano, waiting,
wakes, explodes in liquid fire;
charred earth chills, grows new.

'Art inspired by music, and music transposed to art'

Music's voices, caged in their painted frames,
cry for freedom, rattle their layered bars,
then pause, linger in quiet corners, draw breath
and burst to life, scattering coloured sound.

'Fifty Bees' at the Black Swan

Inspired by Lydia Needle's Frome exhibition 'Fifty Bees – The Interconnectedness Of All Things', February 2020

I've always cherished nature, planted trees,
recorded every moth and butterfly,
devoted earnest hours to garden birds' IDs,
watched goldfinches warm-eyed,
and vowed next year to learn the British hoverflies.

So I'm drawn to 'Fifty Bees', with its art-work pairings
and tidy pedagogy: Linnean binomials,
alluring vernacular names, scraps of natural history.
A scholarly world, a touch arcane – there's not one bee
on the Rodden Nature Reserve's species list.

I find a bee's evolved for every niche.
Crafts and skills are all the buzz – wood-carving,
leaf-cutting, scissoring, masonry and mining.
Diversity rules: wander or stay put; work or laze;
build, defend, pollinate; plunder and predate.

Meanwhile outdoors, on shivering winter days,
snug in cell or nest, the garden bees
lie latent in their sequenced stages,
dreaming gene-obediently of summer honey,
wax and venom, propolis or royal jelly.

Can the bees be helped to thrive in our shared world,
and win back their vanished wild?
Worth a try. I grow the lawn grass floral-meadow high,
favour scented, nectar-bearing, pollen-laden blooms,
choose plants for the friendly shape of their flowers.

I begin to know each bee by its coded colours,
build bug hotels, 'All bees welcome',
flick away the white crab spiders
in ambush on the buddleias,
break cobwebs and free the struggling ravelled catch.

Yes, instinct prevails, outweighs impartial reason:
I choose, unfairly, to take sides with the bees.

Black Swan Arts Young Open 2020

The Young Open is an annual competition for young artists aged 8 – 19. In spring 2020, the usual exhibition was accessible only as a virtual tour.

When my body's trapped in lockdown,
my mind slips free from its quiet shadow
and flies where colour, birdsong, sweet herbs grow
to my senses' secret garden:

chiaroscuro, lavish dawn,
Easter blossom pink in slabbed impasto,
bees shouldering the fruit trees' petalled snow,
crow-black dolmens picking the lawn.

But if that natural idyll palls,
and I crave the artifice of paint and ink,
young art brings fresh delights by virtual link,
emblazoning the Black Swan's walls.

Embrace

For Hiro Takahashi

She begins with the rough crank clay
teased and rolled into coils,
cut into lengths of stiff grey yarn,
plaited into climbing tresses.

In her hands the skein takes form,
ivy clinging to a stump,
the stems entwined, parallel,
bent into folded curves.

Once fired the shape is fixed.
Her fingers trim the clay,
accent the detail, pick out in glaze
the half-seen image in her mind.

With the second firing, the clay reveals
her vision – conjoined arms and hands,
peeping faces, grazing hares,
a baby nestling in the shaded hood.

Serene in the highest hollow
the little one looks out,
sheltered by the safe embrace
of the interwoven strands.

Car Boot at Standerwick

Terza rima

The market's humming – who knows, just might be
the day to find rare treasures and romance;
less buy, more learn – a university.

My mental atlas charts the provenance
of pots from Russia, Holland, Spain, Iran;
Deruta, Wedgwood, Scheurich, Poole, Provence.

Do I know the script? Chinese, Korean,
Japanese? Farsi, Thai, Cyrillic, Greek?
Studio or factory, art or function?

My hands rediscover their sensor knack,
smart fingers scanning jugs, a dish, a bowl;
is there a chip, a mended rim, a crack?

Alluring vase in hand, I sketch the whole,
note colour, glaze, design, the form, the flow;
jot down dimensions, potter's stamp and style.

Maybe I'll try an offer, if I know
we'll feel the same, vase and I, tomorrow.

Poets: A Random Pantheon

Terza rima

My shelf of random spines: there's Blake and Moore,
Chaucer, Byron, Coleridge, Swinburne, Blunden,
three Thomases, Keats, Roethke, Baudelaire,

Pushkin, Wordsworth, Meynell, Housman, Auden,
Shakespeare and Dryden, Browning, Dickinson,
MacLeish – classics, scant chopped prose among them.

What's to learn from this gappy Pantheon?
To write, to convince, must poets suffer
first the muse's dark kiss of loss and pain?

No. Light the heart's flame, though that's tougher
than gloom. Weave flowers to span ekphrastic
bridges, art to words, soft from rougher.

Mould the metre, leave each line elastic,
squeeze rhythms, alliterate the assonance,
dress your images in words still plastic,

encode the palimpsest to spark the sense.
Why write if all you want is self-defence?

Every Inch A King

An acrostic sonnet for William Shakespeare

Each time the tragedy lights up the stage,
Viewed afresh, Act One seems to get it right;
Even King Lear, content in his old age,
Relaxes, smiles, though soon bright day turns night.

Yet destiny, in truth, can still be swung
If Lear will listen to brave Kent's advice.
No chance – too stricken by his daughter's tongue;
Cordelia's sisters glibly vaunt their lies.

His mind in tatters, locked out in the storm,
All friends dismissed, dark Edmund in full sway,
Kin betraying kin, blinding, murder, doom,
In battle beaten, prison's grim array.

No rescue for the once-proud death-ripe king;
God grant such solace as Act Five may bring.

Trompe-l'oeil at Chatsworth

Jan van der Vaardt's 'Portrait of a Violin' (ca. 1723)

The music room door opens to a different world.
Not the illusion of a church dome that leads to heaven,
nor a painted colonnade or theatre backdrop:
instead, the unsafe certainty of ordinary objects.

I steal across the music room, open the door,
reach for the violin hanging on the ribboned disc:
dullish wood, slack strings, a tassel of gut by the tuning pegs,
longish neck, shortish waist, no chinrest.

Not, perhaps, a chef-d'oeuvre by the Master of Cremona;
Stradivari, then in his golden age, might have made
longer 'f' holes, used denser wood or richer varnish,
fashioned a larger body, a more elegant waist.

But I still want to lift it down, slip out the bow, tune the strings,
essay Vivaldi's new music, trace the single line of melody,
hear the thinness of strings in two dimensions,
clap the painter's artifice with one believing hand.

Luncheon of the Boating Party

Aline Charigot, shown with her dog among friends in his 1881 painting, later became Pierre-Auguste Renoir's wife.

I heard the dipping of the oars on the water,
I heard carriage wheels, the soft clip-clop of horses,
I heard clinking glasses, the banter, the laughter.

I saw the crowded terrace, dresses, hats and coats,
I saw the greenery, the beards, the bright faces,
I saw Aline with her pup and, beyond, the boats.

I touched her glass, pretending to be the waiter,
I touched her hand, as if by casual accident;
I touched her heart with a smile, she told me later.

I wondered how, amid that crush, to paint her scent.

Requiem: The Arts Endure

An anthem for Remembrance Day

You knew a time of peace and love,
labour and rest, each day a prayer,
nature's sweet song, life's melody,
discords resolved in harmony.

Yet light and truth did not prevail.
You saw the land laid waste by war;
dark night of infamy and lies –
you chose the path of sacrifice.

Your days cut short by senseless strife,
too brief to learn the craft of life,
for us you paid a bitter price;
now we must rebuild paradise.

Paint battlefields in harvest gold,
forge weapons into tools for good,
fashion pots from the trench's clay,
echo in music each glad day.

V
JEOPARDY

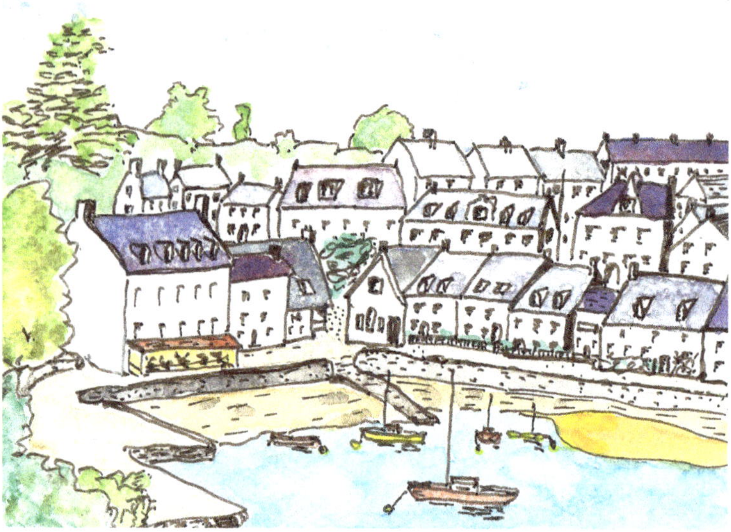

No Child is a Lighthouse

In tribute to John Donne

No child is a lighthouse,
able to stand alone, secure in every storm;
every child is equal, elemental,
a part of one geology.
If the smallest stone be dashed away by the tide of circumstance,
our heartland is the less,
as if a cliff edge crumbled into the sea,
as if the waves swallowed thy friend's estate
or thine own home and family.
Any child's grief diminishes me,
because we are each father or mother to every child.
And therefore never ask for whom the call in time of need;
the call's for thee.

We Three Camels

Fact is, there's stuff you have
to do if you're one of those camels
prophets dream about.

So we slogged west across dreary leagues
of sand and rocks and shingle,
because it was written.

Could have been tougher. Wise men don't carry
much baggage; we three plodded on
with just the magi and their gifts,

often at night – they seemed to need
to see the stars. At last, Herod in Jerusalem,
and on to Bethlehem.

There our riders let us ruminate
while they sought the child. We didn't
expect to see them prostrated.

Gifts given, adoration done,
we slipped away, secretly, the magi
hurried, fearful, all too wise.

We're back east now in Persia, Melchior's country.
Caspar and Balthazar are moving on:
rumours of danger, not really camels' business.

How We're Feeling on the Ark

Yes, Noah was telling the brutal truth:
creation failed, it's a world of sinners.
So, drown the lot, all but Noah's clan, start again;
we animals, sin-free, were just collateral kill.

If he'd been wrong, we'd wasted time, no worse;
if right, we thought, our species might survive.
Would we have boarded if we'd more than half believed
his story? Surely we'd have chosen all to die.

Noah spoke our tongues and we went along.
He kept his word: rescue, food, shelter, truce.
We're in our separate pens; even the lions eat hay.
The ark's as big as a field, four floating storeys tall.

It was no prize to be picked, two by two;
seemed more like sentencing for sacrifice,
condemned to endure a bitter diaspora,
no clinging hope of seeing our native kind again.

On board, each takes it in a different way:
calm elephants and panicky monkeys,
still koalas, restless foxes, snakes and swallows,
touchy rhinos, giraffes and skittish antelopes.

Dark below deck, ringed by endless water,
we shield our private space to nurse our grief.
Will we ever see dry land? And find our way home?
What will home be, all life gone, bereft of our tribes?

Counting the Days

Selflessly, Jonathan
('Call me Jon')
Scantle-Wiles is continuing his sterling work for charity.
Stored in a biscuit tin, Jon has a collection of a hundred
and thirteen shirt buttons culled from discarded garments
over the years – he's a careful fifty-eight.

Jon has vowed to count his buttons
three hundred times
every day while the pandemic lasts. He calculates
he can thereby reach a million
counted buttons in less than four months. He stresses he

isn't doing this for fame or personal profit. 'If I can contribute
in some small way
to better the lives of so many on the front line,
that will be more than enough reward.'
Donations are reportedly mounting apace.

Jon isn't sure if his counting project is an art or a science and
confesses he doesn't
really care: 'it's the result that counts', he contends.

Looking ahead, Jon's next project, still in the planning stage, is
to list the buttons
in his collection by name every week. As he gets to know
them he's becoming familiar with the personality
and individuality of each: 'Their differences,
their idiosyncrasies, but – even more important –
their commonalities, symbolise for me
all that's good in our society'.

He believes that with the aid of modern technology
the project can be world-beating. He's convinced that such
    projects should
be executed locally, in the community, and not
outsourced. He plans to plant a native
hornbeam sapling for each completed list. Needless
to say, he's standing for Parliament.

The Elections: Can Jon Win?

A modest man, justly so he jokes,
Jonathan Scantle-Wiles is not
going out on a limb: the whole
point of elections, like any other sport,
is that winning isn't guaranteed.
Democracy – he confides his simple faith – is
'incredibly important'.

The narrative began almost at birth;
in babyhood,
would it be too bold to imagine
Jon, lying in his cot, tirelessly plotting
his career, his speeches, his
Wikipedia entry, in a manner that was
'incredibly far-sighted'?

The conversation soon turned, even
in boyhood,
to shared core values. In cliché territory,
Jon has trodden carefully; duty to the people
and responsibility to the social contract –
in his discourse these two pillars are always
'incredibly central'.

As to the future, never far away
in adulthood,
it will define itself. Jon stands on a single
platform: to 'listen to the science',
which he sees as unfailingly logical,
politically agnostic, and
'incredibly transparent'.

Refined by repeated political debate
in older maturity,
and knowing that he's right, he refuses compromise:
'if principle leads to conflict, so be it'.
If he must choose between country and principles,
he will unswervingly choose both.
Dewy-eyed at the simple beauty of it, he's
'incredibly patriotic'.

VI
THE HARD YEARS

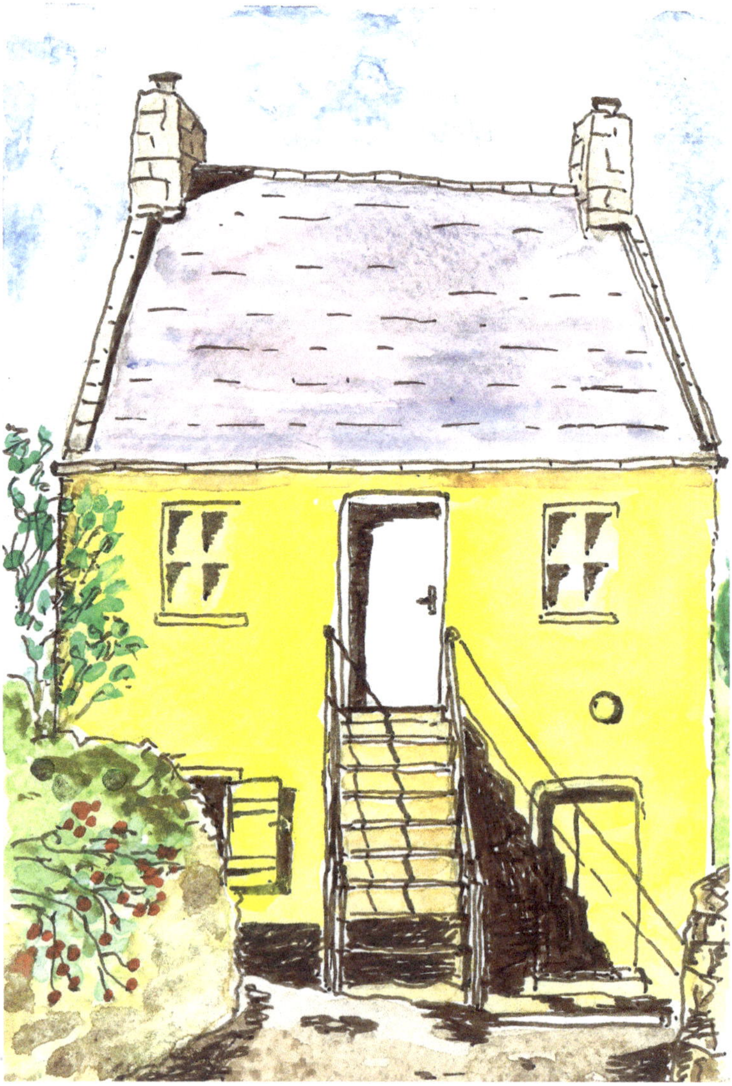

Self-isolation

Sonnet written on 14-15 March 2020

We washed our hands and nodded as the soap
foamed, tossed our soggy tissues in the bin.
This was a battle we could clearly win;
with social distancing we'd surely cope.

But, nothing useful on the medicine shelf,
no vaccine or worthwhile antiviral.
Thousands of cases – a mounting spiral –
so stay home now and isolate yourself!

And then? Learn a language, re-find old friends,
clean out cupboards, dig the garden, shovel
compost, paint a picture, write a novel,
drink prosecco till the crisis ends.

Fragments of herds without immunity,
we'll shelter from our own community.

Getting Ready for Zoom

Mirror, inert, not quite the laptop's camera
but near enough. I play the pin-the-feature game,
shaping the beard to change the face.
More chin? Sideburns? 'Tache?
The beauty of it – I can start again, be another,
with a few days' growth.

The top will do, the inch of T-shirt OK,
the sweater tastefully dull.
I comb the snow-cap cutting the mirror's sky,
my eyes schuss down the face's ridges.
Tiny hiss of Cologne for morale,
then I move, sit, click, clear my throat.

The host admits me, demure
above the line, anything goes below.
I essay finger-tip power:
stop the video, tilt the screen,
appear, disappear, be this me, be
someone other, somewhere else.

Ten Haiku: A Sequence for the Times

Just made six bookmarks.
I dip into piles of books,
can't focus on one.

What were you thinking,
Noah, saving viruses
while unicorns drowned?

Raiding town gardens
after the snow, fieldfares carve
frost-softened apples.

Clear skies, March sunlight –
my shadow's back, breathing drifts
of blackthorn blossom.

East, double rainbow;
west, red-hot coals of sunset;
colours of lockdown.

You're not lost: hold hands,
raise your eyes to spring, follow
the daffodil path.

Second jab cancelled,
used for someone else's first;
two lives protected.

Doctor, your brusque voice
belies your gentle hands – love
your gift of the jab.

Throw the windows wide,
breathe the green, sap-scented air,
sing back to the birds.

Sun-kissed days, soft nights
to come. When we can touch, we'll
make new memories.

Where Sound Should Live

I feel the closeness of the absent sound,
the tight accord of noiseless harmony;
a mix of mingled silences that casts
no shadow on the wall of soundlessness.

By day, sounds outside penetrate the house –
the neighbours' dogs and revving motorbikes,
the railway in the valley, cries of gulls –
displacing half-remembered melodies.

At night it's not quite silent – hearing's more
acute with other senses in repose:
small sounds of wind and rain and bursting plants,
as though the casual dust from fallen stars.

And other missing presences leave gaps
where sound should live in every silent space.
The silence lies like water, undisturbed,
unheard, no person here to move and breathe.

Now

Solitude, silence.
Throw your flint voice in the pool.
Don't expect a splash.

Life is not the same,
life is not the difference;
life lies in between.

A void. Between yes-
terday and tomorrow, no-
thing; let's call it *now*.

The absent present,
bridging the past, the future;
faint scent of roses.

Let's All Grab a Jab

Ballad written end November 2020

If you're out of six-packs
and retracing your tracks
to pick up a beer in the city,
stick tight to the rules,
no truck with the fools
who'll party all night, more's the pity.

Don't take a risk
For the sake of a frisk,
think safety and focus your fears.
With 'Hands, Face and Space'
and 'Test, Track and Trace',
we'll make lockdown burst into tiers.

To harass the virus
and squeeze the disease,
the best shot we've got's vaccination.
If we all play the thug
we'll soon mug the bug:
let's all grab a jab for our nation.

Ordinary Things To Do Again

Plant a Merryweather damson, inhale the blossom, harvest
   the fruit, simmer spicy pickles;
Admire the Judas tree in flower, but reject its merciless
   legend;
Walk the Saturday Market, rifling the Fruit & Veg for the
   choicest, freshest, rarest;
Do the rounds of the charity shops, and maybe find another
   plate from Vallauris;
Sit through 'A Midsummer Night's Dream', tolerate the
   silliness, believe in the magic, relish the actors' words
   and fun;
Sample the steaming vat of carrot and ginger soup in the
   Village Hall kitchen;
Fill a bag with cake and lovingly preserved strawberry and
   Victoria plum from the Friends of St George's;
Sing Allegri's 'Miserere', high soprano perched with the
   angels in the Christ Church organ loft;
Remember the departed at the Last Post, moved to gleaming
   eye by the Town Band trumpeter.